About th

Margaret Beaver is a seventeen-year-old high school senior who began writing at the age of eight and has since partnered that with interests in photography, illustration, and tutoring fellow classmates in the algorithms of literature. She currently resides in her hometown of Plano, Texas, and can be found browsing in any local bookstore. Accompanying her first novel, *Flowers for Papa*, *Seasons: August's Collection* is her second poetry collection, written between the ages of fifteen and sixteen. You can follow her literary ventures on Instagram @_margaretbeaver_ , and for insight into her next works, visit her at margaretbeaverbooks.com.

SEASONS
AUGUST'S COLLECTION

Margaret Beaver

SEASONS
AUGUST'S COLLECTION

Vanguard Press

VANGUARD PAPERBACK

© Copyright **2024**
Margaret Beaver

The right of Margaret Beaver to be identified as author of this work has been asserted by her in accordance with the Copyright, Designs and Patents Act 1988.

All Rights Reserved

No reproduction, copy or transmission of this publication may be made without written permission.
No paragraph of this publication may be reproduced, copied or transmitted save with the written permission of the publisher, or in accordance with the provisions of the Copyright Act 1956 (as amended).

Any person who commits any unauthorised act in relation to this publication may be liable to criminal prosecution and civil claims for damages.

A CIP catalogue record for this title is available from the British Library.

ISBN 978 1 80016 716 2

*Vanguard Press is an imprint of
Pegasus Elliot Mackenzie Publishers Ltd.*
www.pegasuspublishers.com

First Published in 2024

**Vanguard Press
Sheraton House Castle Park
Cambridge England**

Printed & Bound in Great Britain

ALSO BY MARGARET BEAVER

inkwells.
A POETRY COLLECTION

Flowers for Papa
A NOVEL

To Shi, for our faults were never timely

A MESSAGE FROM THE AUTHOR

Seasons: August's Collection is the poetic and lyrical amalgamation of references to events and statements both old and new, both presented in the original work of *Flowers for Papa* and not. This work is to be told from the perspective of August Johnson, though some individual poems within this work do not pertain directly to August, but rather August's imagination, as, of course, we all have one of those.

There is specific subject matter and blunt language used at sparse intervals throughout the work, and this message will be the *only* trigger warning incorporated so as to not wrongfully gauge which poems may or may not be triggering according to an individual reader, and to not disrupt the flow of the work. As always, I urge any and all readers to confront any negative feelings which may, understandably, be triggered due to the dark themes, and discontinue reading this work should the subject matter become too impactful.

This work is a blend of both authentic and realistic notions and themes secured with the comprehensive fictionality of August's character and the entirety of the *Flowers for Papa* characters. Under no circumstances should any reader compromise their nonfiction mental health for a very much fictional character. August would not want you to.

Be safe and well,
Margaret Beaver

TABLE OF CONTENTS

ALSO BY MARGARET BEAVER / 6
A MESSAGE FROM THE AUTHOR / 8
i told you to run away / 15
hurt people hurt people / 18
outgrowing / 21
blood rivers / 22
flower man / 28
it's going swimmingly / 30
my umbrella / 33
lungs / 36
christmas day in the rain / 41
the pharmacy / 44
the art of being paper happy / 48
angels in disguise / 52
it's a long road to walk alone / 56
love as written but never said / 59
away: the words of a panic attack / 63
starving / 65
chasing atlantis / 68
the garden & the grave / 73
halfheartedly / 77
serotonin, dopamine, anything / 81
circling / 84
spring cleaning / 87
supernovas don't scare me anymore / 91

broken glass / 96
the ill-mannered gentleman / 100
better / 104
patience / 108
the chain / 112
yellow / 117
an inch of religion / 121
hiding places / 125
seasons / 132
papa's poem (bonus) / 133
FEELING SUICIDAL? / 139

i told you to run away

Your hair falls above your ears
The times had all but frozen
But there's no fear
And you're the past
And you're ever so alive

I rest my head on my hands
Eyes closed, playing with the stain on your pants
Your head is tired of aching and your throat is tired of burning
And I am tired of you yearning
For something that's not there
To wander the woods, treading on your soul of ice,
And wonder why the trees are bare
Should you come to before the sun does sleep,
You would see
My flesh is splintered a masterpiece
From how your shards do seethe

The more I learn about myself, the more I hate myself
Spend our days drowning in the cards you've been dealt
And your finger circles the stain

Like our minds circle the drain
A strange way for our demons to die
But at least they're dead

I let you spend the night
You let you spend your life
Dreaming the fantasies of a queen's maid
She lost her broom, and we're the wandering souls who
Never wander home
Maybe we are the seeds of flowers
That will never grow
We are the ones who love
But never show
We are so lonely
Never alone

The fire dried the stain
And now you are awake
It's time for me to run,
But never away

hurt people hurt people

I've gone to far too many funerals
The faces look the same
Keep telling the kids they can't come home
If they could feel, they'd feel estranged
We tie our nooses a little tighter
When we think of the mess we made
Our webs of scars—no, they're our art
And you feel the need to paint

Keep wandering these corridors
As the chains settle around my dreams
The rope is frayed more than that day
But it's nothing I can't believe
A coach man sat in a first-class seat,
For he was never very bright
If you had seen the things I'd seen,
You wouldn't sleep without a light

The sinks are clogged
But the blood runs like the water can no longer
I cannot feel you, but my brain memorized the touch
I outline the burn circles as I ponder

I've seen who you are, but you have not,
For you still stand in front of the mirror
But press my face up to the glass
While my limbs lie drowning in the river

The tap is cold, the smells are wet
Don't act like I don't remember,
For I do float above the stream
And think of nights of burning embers

We are merely an extension of who we admire in our minds
Mixed with the dimming lights of old freight cars and faking alibis;
You must imagine devils dancing on the throats of children wishing on shooting stars,
Must come running to a halt to catch a taste of good blood,
For you are not half the man you think you are

And all the lights wink out
Just for a moment, I am lost and found
My eyes hold still behind my eyelids now
These waters have come to cure my drought

And all the lights wink out
Just for a moment, I am lost and found
My eyes hold still behind my eyelids now
Why do hurt people hurt people?

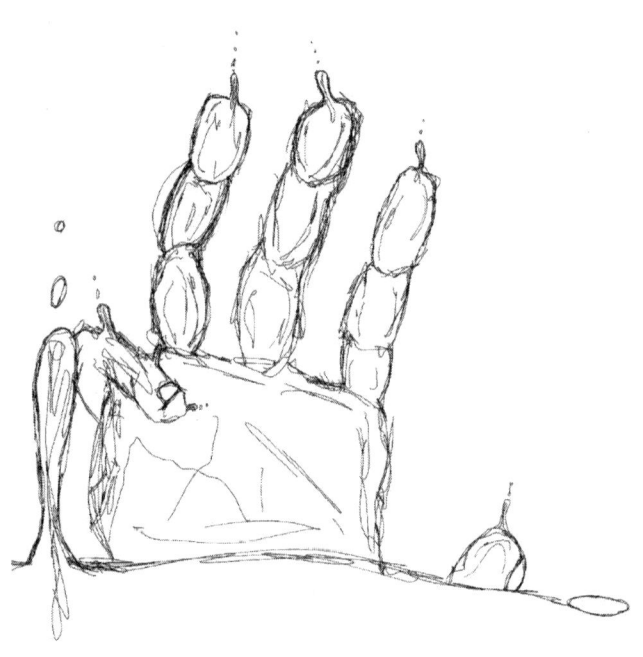

outgrowing

I've been up all night, doing everything to learn my lines
And perhaps if I drill it in I won't have to think twice
But it's a battle of kings who are all masochists
They'd all rather fall than live
To beg someone to stay when they should want to
Is to grow up dreaming of worlds you'll only outgrow

Wonder when I'll live like that
Walking in the sand, guiltless of my tracks
Staring at the skies and never looking back
I'd like to see the day
When I'm standing in the rain again
Singing all the songs instead of humming inside my head
I'll see you when I come back

Because I don't wanna be here
I miss being excited about life
I miss never thinking twice
I miss you

I'm so tired of chasing dreams

Penny for your thoughts just between you and me
I'd pull all your teeth just to hear you scream
Because I don't wanna be here

You don't have to dream of me
As long as I'm the one you see before falling asleep
I need to heal before I hurt you
But emptiness and I are very old friends
And then there was silence and a bit of regret
Because I don't wanna be here

But I'm afraid you washed away in the tide
Thank you for being what I needed and all my reasons why
Looking back, I can't even remember what we were running from
I hope you didn't think I'd think you'd stay
Because I don't wanna be here
It was only when I became my own home
That I realized this house was burning
And in these flames you can't see me

My mind's telling me to let go
But I don't wanna be alone
Now you're walking the town all on your own
And when we lock eyes and you frown, I'll know you know
Growing up dreaming of worlds you'll only outgrow
Because I don't wanna be here

blood rivers

It's fun craving pain
At least then I'm always satisfied
I might miss you; I might love you; I might try so hard to keep you
But it's the only thing I keep:
I keep on craving pain

It's been a while since you went away
It's been a while, but it feels the same
And it's a shame I never asked you more
About what you wanted to become one day
Because I hope it wasn't this

For I bathe in the blood of the breakers of hearts
And their bones pick flesh from my teeth
The shadow worker slowly turns out their light
I finally enjoy the screams

For I would never let your creative eyes go blind
Hell to pay if your ends never meet
I will not starve you
But you will sit at the table

And watch me eat

Did you feel loved?
Because you were loved
Was the love not enough or were you not enough?
It's when you become the very thing you swore to
destroy evidence of,
I think that's when you pull the trigger of that empty,
empty gun
These rivers aren't dry;
They're full of blood

For I bathe in the blood of the breakers of hearts
And their bones pick flesh from my teeth
The shadow worker slowly turns out their light
I finally enjoy the screams

For I would never let your creative eyes go blind
Hell to pay if your ends never meet
I will not starve you
But you will sit at the table
And watch me eat

Did you feel loved?
Because you were loved
Was the love not enough or were you not enough?
It's when you become the very thing you swore to
destroy evidence of,

I think that's when you pull the trigger of that empty,
empty gun
These rivers aren't dry;
They're full of blood

flower man

In a hurricane,
I wouldn't be able to place
If I were the crashing waves
Or the innocent buds ripped from their roots

In a meteor shower,
Would the stars be the ones dancing in your eyes
Or would they be the ones falling from the skies—
Do you think they regret the nights that it felt right?

And all the children, they watch
They don't want to be something they'll forget
But they don't know what else to be
As they bleed every time they breathe
And all the ships, they just watch them sink

They scrambled to build an island in this tide
But they set sail on their ocean eyes
The only things the children had was everything they gave away
If they could give it back, I don't think they'd give the pain
Singing, oh, love kills

But we die anyway

In the end,
We're all just children forced to play a role
We didn't audition for
So I will be the man
To grow in this downpour

Mother, why doesn't he smile with his eyes?
Because he's a flower man
Mother, why does he smile with his mind?
Because he's a flower man

With lips of dragon's blood and no eyes to see,
His pores, they sprout with bay-born posies
And the big thick stump
In which his head was crushed
Grows buds and leaves and sprout-like things
His crown, a pool for children to swim with water wings
A playground of ghostly underwater forest trees
Singing, oh, you must be a florist
Bringing color to everything

And they always ask the questions, Can you see me?
I am blind but I can see you
Can you hear me?
I am deaf but I can hear you
Can you feel me?

I am numb but I can feel you
Can I be me?
Can I be a flower man?

I scrambled to build an island in this tide
But they set sail on my ocean eyes
The only things I had was everything I gave away
If I could give it back, I don't think I'd give the pain
Singing, oh, love kills
But we die anyway

it's going swimmingly

Bad thoughts feel heavy
But they're light;
They never sink to the bottom of the sea
But I thought I could hold them down
If I painted my bedroom green

I bought some fake flowers and giraffe figurines
And hung my kitty his very own stocking
But I wish I were somewhere else
At the bottom of the sea

Is it a poison, or is it a peace?
Is it inside me, or underneath?
Maybe I could sink
And come back if it's too much
If the sharks find me wandering
The water streets
If on the way down, my bad thoughts start haunting me
But no one will hear me scream
At the bottom of the sea

My heart's an old balloon

Still in my closet from February
If I could say something, it'd probably be an apology
Because I took you and I ruined you
And I'm sorry
But I'll see you at the bottom of the sea

I bought new paintings, and, in the shower, I sing
And I even got a few more piercings
But I still wish I were somewhere else
But I'll keep walking this town in the spring
With a mind at the bottom
Of the sea

my umbrella

I am the one who stood under the gutters, soaking in
the flush of rain
I am the one wishing for amnesia to erase the things I
say
I am the broken umbrella melting several landfills
away—
From home

I am someone who can teach you how to be lonely too
I am someone who hasn't repaid the debts well
overdue
I am someone who pinched the flesh just to quench the
craving
I am someone giving private lessons on how to speak
while shaking

Some say I see myself in dirty mirrors; that's why I
write in the dark
That I purposely plant trees just to struggle climbing
the bark
The only love I ever had was a love that drained like
old rain

And I broke my umbrella trying to get you to stay

I am the one sitting in the darkest corner of the house
I am the one who killed the bud so the plant wouldn't sprout
I sit drinking from someone's dirty ashtray
Everybody looks up when they call my name
I just adjust my mask; it's a masquerade

And I am the one who goes home alone
And blames myself in the bed of my hometown
I never outgrew the playground,
Nor the bullies
I see myself in dirty mirrors
So I'll keep writing in the dark
I am the one who's told to turn it down
And blame myself in the bed of my hometown
The only love I ever had was a love that drained like old rain
And I broke my umbrella trying to get me to stay

I wish I fixed my umbrella before I threw it away

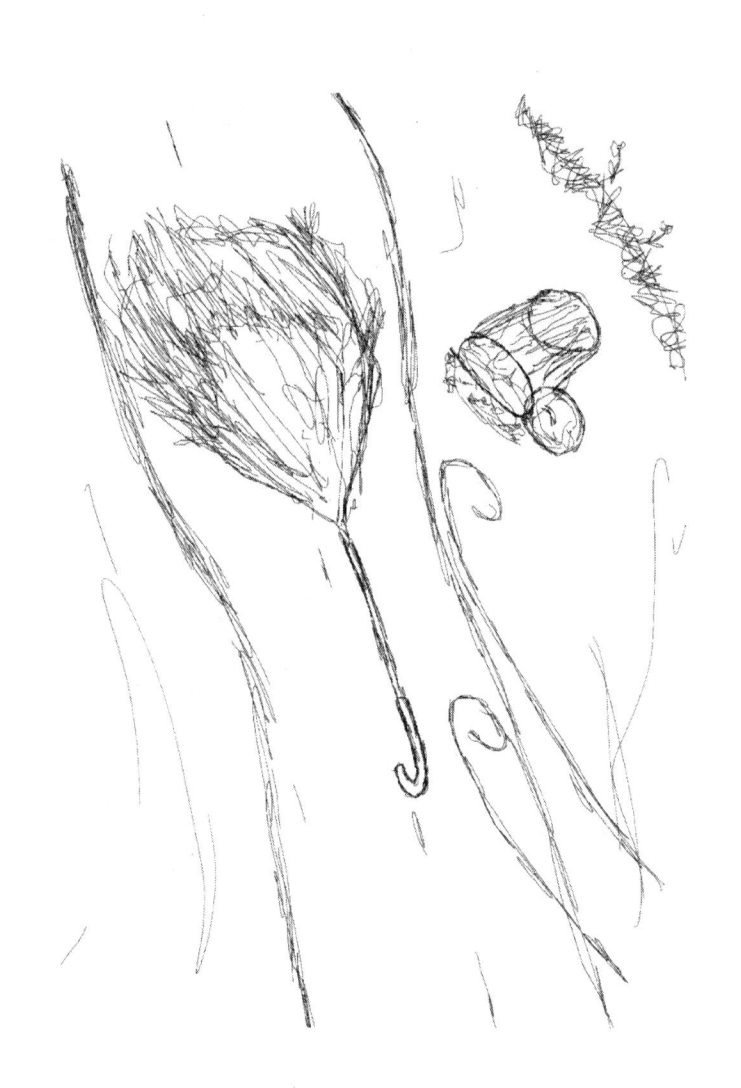

lungs

Emotions bottled in the windows
Of the stores I can't afford
I walk the gravel roads as a barefoot peasant girl
As young as the morning,
A mind as dark as autumn leaves
Tiny hands holding onto the fear
That everybody will leave me

I would relight an old flame
But relit cigarettes never taste the same
And she is the only one
Who could save my lungs,
The girl selling reasoning for three a piece
A walking remedy, lovesickness is the only ill
She can't cure

And I walk, awake enough to know what's going on
But too asleep to know what it means
Oh, it must be the void consuming me
I pass the cobblestone square;
The wind cradles her hair
And I watch from a dark lamppost

A sad smile for my fingers' unanswered wish

Long before zoning, Mama had told me,
The builders had placed a bridal shop next to a church
And I can't help but thinking—well, more like dreaming—
that maybe we could be the first

The priest may never marry us
Hell could empty in the church
But I can still hold her like she's the only thing
That ever made me feel alive
I can still love her like she is
All my reasons why
I am living this life in person
Rather than seeing it from the sky

Perhaps in another life we'd have been lovers
Perhaps in another life we'd have saved each other
She could stand in the dark and I'd see her without a shadow
And it's the least I could do,
For giving me a tomorrow

Her mother called at one o'clock
Her voice rang through the air
I was trading a scotch for some winter socks
But her shriek made the last full trees go bare
A reserved woman, I was shocked to hear her scream

I had heard enough yelling to know when someone was making a scene
I turned to see her daughter placed upon a wooden block
In the middle of the square
The townsfolk gathered around the women, yelling numbers
And the very last autumn leaf died there

I'm only a single feather in her wing of life
But it's okay; I've been waiting my whole life to die
But before I go, I just want you to know
If you were the sun, you'd be eclipsed
And I would gladly bloody my knuckles for the rest of you to exist

The priest never married us
Hell had emptied in the church
And I never got to hold her like she's the only thing
That ever made me feel alive
I never got to love her like she is
All my reasons why
I never got to lay with her until the day
I died

I would relight an old flame
But relit cigarettes never taste the same
And she was the only one
Who could save my lungs

From the void that came
On the bidding day

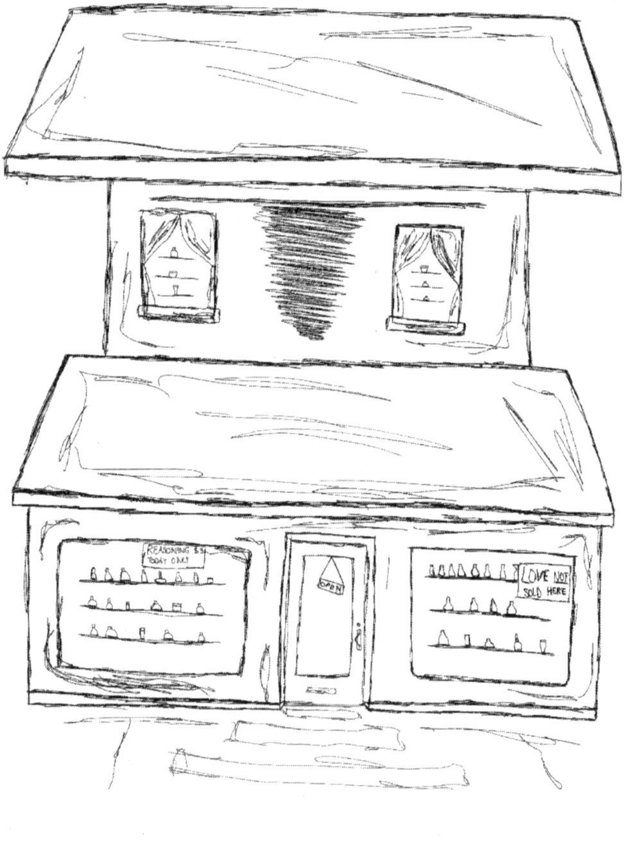

REASONING $3
TODAY ONLY
OPEN
LOVE NOT SOLD HERE

christmas day in the rain

Thank you for the Christmas Eves when everything
went wrong
Thank you for the little songs that you sing to the dogs
Thank you for setting spring in my mind of winter fog
Thank you for being everything I needed
When I was weak, and you were strong

If only lovers die, then I'll be there in the cold
Sitting in the empty pew of the church, listening alone
I'll be there when they tell all the stories that have
already been told
And on my lips, it's not my tears I'll be tasting;
I'll taste every chocolate kiss from your stash that I
stole

I'll think of all the bright blues and greens and reds
you paint with all the time
And every rocky mountain from the ground that I
watched you climb
I know that every time I close my eyes, that life will be
all right

Because I'm certain your birth had made the universe align

If I hadn't mentioned it already,
I would spend Christmas Day in the rain with you
There are still certain things I can't say out loud,
But I'm hoping one day I'll come through
And I will tell you all the things you probably already assumed
But for now, you have a piece of me
And I have all of you

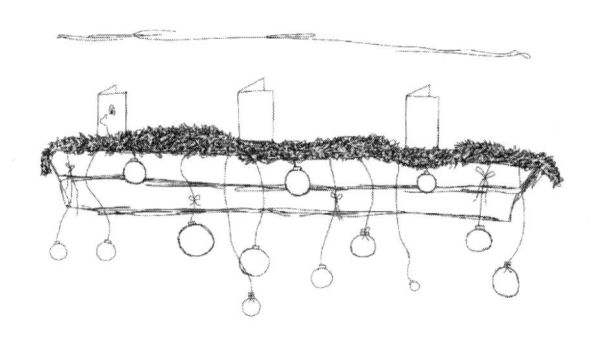

the pharmacy

(I drank the poison for you
But the poison was you
And now I know the truth
As I'm dying)

My stomach is a pharmacy
And my meds have been stolen
My stomach is the pharmacy
On the gray side of town,
Where the glass lies broken
The registers aren't open but they're empty inside
And this pharmacy is sick
Just like the patients with sick minds

This pharmacy has files ten feet tall
I don't know the people, but I know their minds
I guess I can't judge when we all have the same intention:
Trying to buy time

Sure, my customers are the dark ones but they're the only ones I like

I never trust the good ones until I know how they got
their light
I used to be one, but they all stole mine
And blamed me for being dark;
They're the type to only love the shards,
Never mind the whole
And I drained the poison from my lovesick stomach
I outgrew all I've been told

I ring you up; it's past your bedtime
Does your mother know you're out at night?
But their soul keeps whispering the questions
I ask myself all the time:
If you loved me,
Why'd you hurt me?
Why'd you sink me
And puncture my lungs so I couldn't be found?
Why'd you cut me
Until I couldn't breathe?
Your stealing me was when I found out
I had something left…

I catch wisps of a wanderer down aisle three:
Everything looks different when it's only you who's
changed
But it's hard to savor the red of autumn
When you're the only one to blame

And more souls come slinking in,

And more thoughts,
And more poison I drink:
I guess I'm one of the lucky ones,
I've not fallen in love with someone I'll never be;
I never fall when I know there's nothing there to catch me

The line trails down the street; I pass the next some morphine
And even the bottles start to sing:
I'm just a drop in the ocean
But you needed that drop to feel complete
I mean, yes, I'm sinking
But the view is
Amazing

(I drank the poison for you
But the poison was you
And now I know the truth
As I'm dying)

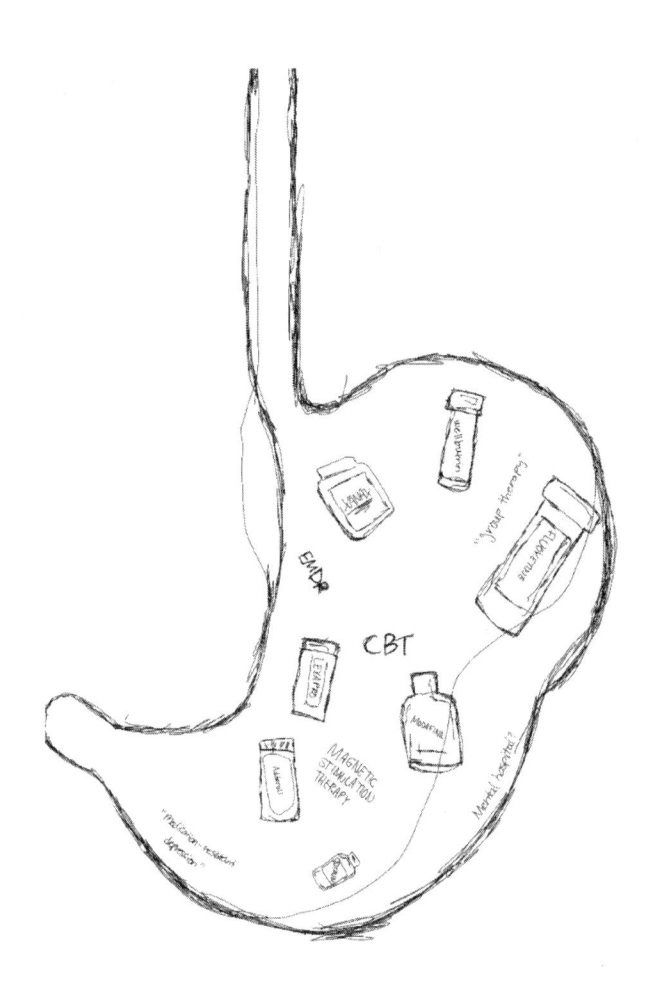

the art of being paper happy

I thought I healed from this
I thought I healed from you
But if I saw me now,
I wouldn't see a flower bloomed
I'd see a reckless heart
I'd see breathing in the dark
I'd see someone who is incomplete
The painter of this masterpiece
Is paper happy

The builder of this home forgot all the windows
I could leave but the dark entices me
I could leave but I have masterpieces to paint
I could leave but I have happiness to give away
And so I traipse up and down the stairs,
Repeating the words that you said
If that's how you hear me in your head,
I understand it now

That you were paper happy
I never thought you'd have to heal from me
But if I saw you now, I wouldn't see a flower bloomed

I'd see a reckless heart
I'd see breathing in the dark
I'd see someone who is incomplete
The painter of this masterpiece
Accidentally drew a sad soul on their best friend
And their blue eyes are paper happy
And those eyes see right through me

Like a mother's womb who couldn't keep caring for the child
Their body promised to nurture
Like a girlfriend's eyes who holds their best friend's hands
And on the playground, they admit
They don't see a future

We all have wounds that will heal
And stomach scars from unborn children
We have wounds that will lock their doors and shut us out
We have wounds that will pack our bags
And kick us out of the house
But these wounds all will heal
Maybe not through time, but through love
And I hope the next time I pick up a paint brush,
I'll paint a happier one

The house took the front door and wedged it open
If we have no windows, lest we have this light

The more I love you, the more I hurt you,
The more I push you away
You are the clean white clouds and I, the sky of gray

But you need me to dance in the rain
And I need you to paint the sky of day

The mother steps through the door and carries
Her child soft to sleep
The basement downstairs is cramped with emerald green eyes
So she takes her brushes and sets up round the crib

We all have wounds that will heal
And stomach scars from unborn children
We have wounds that will lock their doors and shut us out
We have wounds that will pack our bags
And kick us out of the house
But these wounds all will heal
Maybe not through time, but through love

And the mother picks up her paint brush,
And paints a happier one

angels in disguise

It's cold outside
Before the fall, you close your eyes
And I'm in bed, thinking how I only say
What I think I should feel
Maybe when I'm dead and gone, they'll sing a song for me
Maybe when I'm dead and gone, it'll be the first song you'll ever sing
Take your coat, I say, because it's cold outside
But not too cold for angels to fly

How the hands that held you are the hands that destroyed you
I never meant to love you, and you never meant to want me to
And I could fill with the drugs in the place of your love
And I could sprout in your spring just to die in my winter
I tried to clip your wings so you couldn't fly
But what if we're both angels in disguise?
What if it's too cold outside?

My head is heavy with all the weight I won't let you carry
You could stand a thousand feet and fall with a single ounce of me
You say it's not my fault but it's never what you mean
I would call but I'm too tired to be free

Our memories are but the smiles of our ghosts
And sticky sands to linger in their time
Of the kids who once walked the beaches
With seashells the colors of their eyes,
Looking for all the things we still cannot find
Because it's cold outside

I have my reasons to stay and my reasons to go
But this bed will be empty by morning, we know
I could lie to myself and say that I tried
When I gave up our world to suffer inside mine
Because how dare you say you know me
When I don't even know myself
I drown in the waters where my demons can swim
And they revive me every time

How the hands that held you are the hands that destroyed you
I never meant to love you, and you never meant to want me to
And I could fill with the drugs in the place of your love

And I could sprout in your spring just to die in my winter
I tried to clip your wings so you couldn't fly
But what if we're both angels in disguise?
What if it's too cold outside?

We drained like the old water of the melting snow
Our bodies bound together on the floor of the rowboat
Under a horizon so far but so close
They're singing the song for you that I wrote

The church people stopped singing their hymns
The day we closed our eyes
The demons revived me every time,
Because what if we're both
Angels in disguise?

it's a long road to walk alone

Sunday morning hearts can't eat at a Friday night feast
The mistress will say to drink the wine, but only if you have the stomach to eat
All the guilt that you will hold; it won't be falling to your feet
But it's too late to leave

We are the creatures of our very worst nightmares
We are the lovers who never found each other
But now we're beyond repair
I could settle at a diner and drink all the wine
But I'm walking home
It's a long road to walk alone

In the early hours, the windows shattered; mother never knew
How to wake the kids without destroying all the flowers they worked to bloom
Out beyond egos and thrones,
There is a field of daisies
They are drooping in the sun; the rain is coming
It is time I walk you home

The stove lit fire in the kitchen
And the water pipes froze
Every instinct I'd ever had was telling me
Our house was dying overgrown
And if there's no home to go home to,
Where am I walking alone?
It's a long road to walk alone

And in your porch light, I'll be screaming,
It's a long road to walk alone
It's a long road
Will you walk me home?

You open the door, and there's your face,
And then I'm home

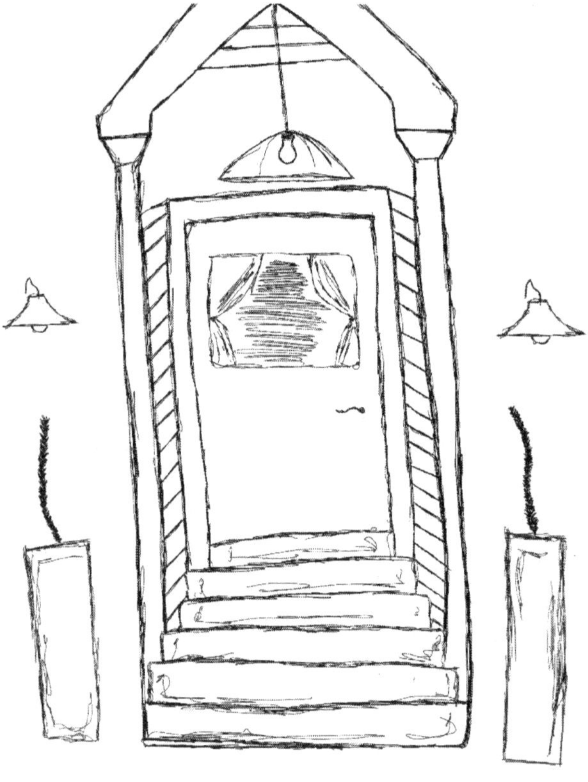

love as written but never said

We were bundled in the car
The night I held you from afar
And told you everything I'll never say again;
The night you told me about your father
And the songs he used to sing that he'll
Never sing again

The little girl grew a garden
And now the woman is surrounded
Except for the squirrel who always used to sniff the
sunflowers
He never comes around any more

And I'd hate to think that when I look at you, I catch a
glimpse
Of the person who uprooted your tree
And I'd hate to think that after months of feeding
lullabies to untrusting children,
They'd finally believe
When no one's left to sing them now

I treasure her face

Her shoulders, which carry the weight
She won't let anyone else
And in my mind I am outlining the freckles on her nose
They're but a fleeting vision, but you're not to me
You never leave,
Even when I want you so bad

Nobody's ever stayed when I felt
Like that

I treasure her shoulders, which carry the weight
She won't let anyone else
Heaven and Hell rest on their opposing sides
And she the only referee to their arguments

And she doesn't deny it when I ask
She says, "Yes, meet my little friends.
This one's Heaven and this is Hell, too."
She dances to Hell's favorite music and reads the books of Heaven,
As only a true war would do

I treasure her scars which cling to skin,
Like medicine,
And I breathe into flesh that's stretched
Behind her knees, trailing down her thighs,
And perhaps in places I have not yet laid my eyes
Nor a hand on

But I'm waiting patiently

I treasure her eyes, in which ships sail up their golden globe—
Not knowing where they're going,
But where they need to be

If you must know, it's a sable fire in which my love has been written,
But never said

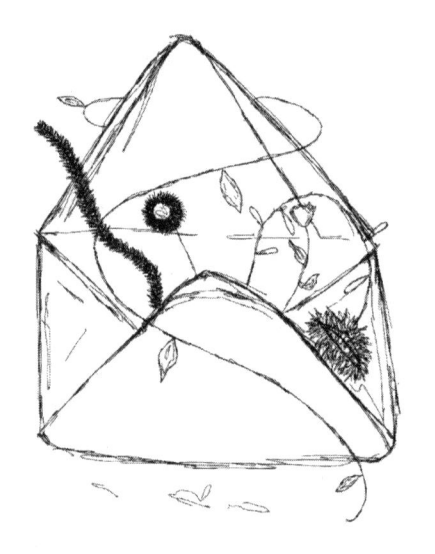

away: the words of a panic attack

i am encased in this sickness.

this body is so limiting; i'm trapped here. i'm trapped in this sickness. i'm trapped in my head. i'm trapped in my stomach. i want to scratch my skin and i bleed and i bleed and i bleed, just to let my soul out. even just a little bit.

i don't want to be here. i need to get out of here. i'm panicking—i'm trapped. i'm screaming inside my head because i can't scream out loud. i've been sick for days—no one can figure out why. my father gave me ptsd—i can't tell him. i disagree. i disagree. i disagree. i don't like it when you tell me you don't want me to look like a boy. just let me cut my hair the way i want it. just let me be the way i want to. i'm keeping so many secrets. i'm pretending i like these people. i'm pretending i'm happy. i'm raging. i'm shaking. i'm wasting. i'm sick. i'm sick in my stomach. i'm sick in my head. i'm burning. i want to burn. i want to strap myself to a stake and burn. so my screaming, out loud, will be the last thing i hear. so i know i can do it.

i want to be away. i have to be away.

AWAY

starving

Do you love me now,
Now that I've finally gotten out?
Out of the floorboards, out of the forest,
But hopefully not out of your head
Can you see it now?
The sunlight gleaming through the trees
They are as tall as my love, but that never seemed to
Mean anything

If I threw a branch, would it break your wings?
So you fall back down and I can speak
Everything I've ever wanted to say
Please don't tell me we speak a different language,
Or is it just you only see me as the tree
That shot you down
And not the tree who wants you around?

I could say anything, but would that mean enough?
I could fight fire with fire, but I don't have the brush
To rebuild and regrow everything we've lost
Would you even want it back?

When you come home late,
I'll stay awake and keep the light on
It might be midnight, but my poem needs a rhyme
Can you see the sunlight through the trees,
Or am I too tall for you to see?

After everything, I think you wished I'd walked away
But I am planted in the ground, the ground you fly over
Every day

How am I supposed to leave? I say
Well, how could you break my wings and think it's okay?

How was I supposed to get you to stay?
I can't even go find food, you complain
But at least you're here, I say,
Starving

The winter comes and I am bare
No coat to keep you warm out here
You start to sink beneath the earth
But at least you're here,
Starving

Maybe if I prop you up just right
You'll stay until the summertime
Why aren't your bird friends looking for you?

It's because they don't care like I do

Your body feeds this earth
And while you're starving, I'm rebirthed
I would thank you but you're not here
To hear the words

How was I supposed to get you to stay?
I can't even go find food, you used to complain
But at least you're here, I claimed,
Starving

chasing atlantis

If this isn't you, then whose vial of ashes am I
wearing?
Have I returned a phantom and burned myself?
Would I have extinguished the flames
If I didn't love the colors so much?
The oranges and reds of fire are the blood of my body,
The blood of the wounds that never bleed

I told you I loved you the day before I left you
I see brighter suns, but only in my dreams
Oh, to have taken my soul of two left feet
And taught it how to dance
Dying is an art only to be perfected once,
But to be practiced for a lifetime
Our ashes seem to grind a little more each day

The day was white when I asked if you would love me
As the fountain of this sinking kingdom:
A worthless, beautiful destruction
If I could pour my acid dreams into my pillowcase
Do you think they'd sink in again?
The children on the train are screaming in glee

But they haven't left the station

To think these kingdoms were as eternal as my love
I was right until holes were shot in the bricks
To think the knights wouldn't drop with the arrows in their chests
But I guess that's what I get for dreaming of
The seeming eternity of hypothetical kingdoms

The witchdoctor was called to town to treat the mass
There wasn't enough medicine for me
So I tread a few short days a flower struggling to bloom
Until a widowed mother shined her sun
And the blood began to run
Not from my chest, but from my head
Deep inside of me

The day was white when I asked if you would love me
As my mind of gunpowder
And lips of a bullet
Who speak words
That only hurt myself

To think these wounds were as eternal as my love
I was right until the queen was carried dead from the broom closet
To think there's enough sun to make all of the blood dry up

But I still bleed, oh, I still bleed
I guess that's what I get for dreaming of
The seeming eternity of chest wounds

If it's not me, then whose vial of ashes am I wearing?
I had found myself in you, love;
I had discovered we are both more than enough
Even if our irony has captured us:
You offered your whole self;
I offered what was left
But we were equals
In that we gave
All we had

But I have a mind of gunpowder
And a soul of a flower eager to bloom
Dying is an art only to be perfected once,
But to be practiced for a lifetime
We are the last star dust trying to find our way back to the sky,
Where chest wounds are some knights' revival
But, sir, I have flowers to water
But they'll be flowers where we're going
Once we leave the station

Even when my head is clearer
And the number is zero,
I'll still dedicate that one second
To counting the people I'll lose

With a mind of gunpowder,
A soul of a flower eager to bloom,
And the blood of my body,
The blood of wounds that never bleed

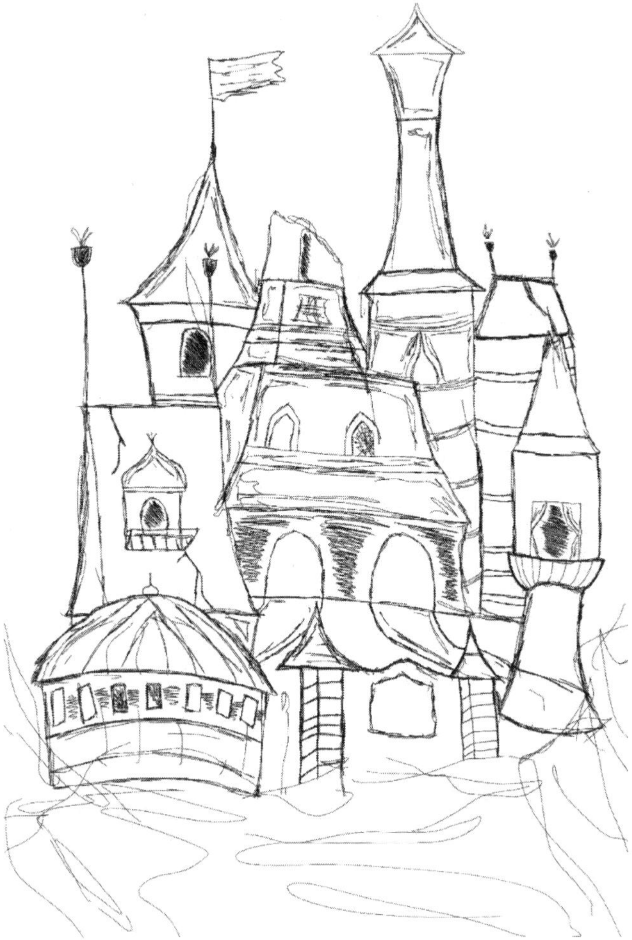

the garden & the grave

If she were a book,
I'd fold her at her corners,
Or slip a bookmark inside her,
Between her pages,
Because there will always be a part of her I want to come back to,
Even if it hollows me to linger
In the chapters of our downfall,
Of our everything that could have been,
Of the meanings that have now gone thin,
Of our everything that actually was,
That my eyes weren't open enough to notice.

The nights spent teaching me to play the violin in a field of canola,
The mornings eager for coffee and that very last sip,
The wordless afternoons in angry air and faces worn
Like the awkward smile a child would draw on their villain—
A face where one doesn't belong.
And still, I continue in the chapters of our battle royal:
It was me, it was you, but it was also our ghosts

Of our everything that could have been,
Of the meanings that have now gone thin,
Of our everything that actually was.
If you put a price on the feeling, I couldn't afford it;
I was too free, and I felt none of it.

It's good weather to stay alive, I suppose,
But you only want the ones you miss the most,
So I'll leave you here in the greenhouse;
The flowers can appease the hunger you feel no more,
Or at least the hunger you feel no more for me.

If she were a bud,
I'd be told to place her deep in the fields of the sun,
But I mustn't, because I'm selfish,
And I'd imagine a little love is better than none.
When she withers, I will not fret about the mess I have made;
I will carry her back to the greenhouse where she'll die miles away.

But I had never known guilt until the regret that crept to me.
You'll be laced in honeysuckle vines by morning;
I'll sink you deep beneath the ghost orchid tree,
So you could see them one last time,
The flowers you will never see again.

When it's time we feed well our earth, you'll be nested in bed,
The homely trinkets of our lives scattered about the house,
As I begin for the door.
I carry flowers in my hands for you, from the garden and the grave.

halfheartedly

In the mornings, we're tangled hearts and unspoken words
And I'm tired
Of wondering who will break first
I thought I'd get you if I tried
But that was another empty lie
And I could wonder why
But I know

Half of my heart has always been yours,
So now I can only say it halfheartedly:
It was with flowers that I broke our promise,
But it was with pain that I let you leave
And I know I do it often
But I guess life just isn't complete
Without a promise or two to break
And letting our garden grow weak

I don't have demons;
I have children in my head
Wondering what they did to make me so sad
And they're flustered

They're pushing every button to reverse what they've done
They don't understand; I am the only one
Who knows if you're not here, there's no reason not to succumb

I am the engineer of my own downfall, with no energy to run

A few years' time
And I am here to tell you I escaped it,
And you remember how you watched me leave
Are you still mad about the promise?
I hope you're not,
But I would be

I am here to tell you I escaped me
The children are fine: they're bathed and clean
But sometimes the nights get darker
And sometimes it's hard to eat

Do you still think about Oklahoma
And the night everything went wrong?
Sometimes I think about Louisiana
And the unanswered calls on your phone
But I'd rather see you in my dreams
Than when I stand in the mirror and our crimes reflect back at me:
You are angry in love, but I'm just

Scared

Half of my heart has always been yours,
So now I say it halfheartedly:
Only come back when you can stay longer
Or when you can promise you won't leave

I never knew "I love you"
Until I wrote it down and scratched it out
On the last six pages of my journal
No one ever reads that far
Without gagging
Or running
Away

serotonin, dopamine, anything

anything that i need
anything that i can reach
but not the pill bottles please
i'm searching for something
serotonin, dopamine,
anything

i'm terrified to let you in
you'll only hurt me again
i'm not the best at making friends
when i do, i just leave you dry
dry like my eyes
no, i won't cry
i'm too trapped inside
there's a fatal disease inside my mind
my hands reach for the shelves but nothing's right
not the pill bottles please
i'm searching for something

i
get lost
i get low

out of here
out of touch
lose my breath
count to ten
i have gone searching
again

for anything that i'll need
when i'm at the doctor's for a week
when i get too frail and you carry me
down the stairs and to the beach
let me see it one last time
i'm too controlled by my mind
i'm searching for something
anything that i can reach

anything that i need
anything that i can reach
but not the pill bottles please
i'm searching for something
serotonin, dopamine,
anything
serotonin, dopamine,
anything

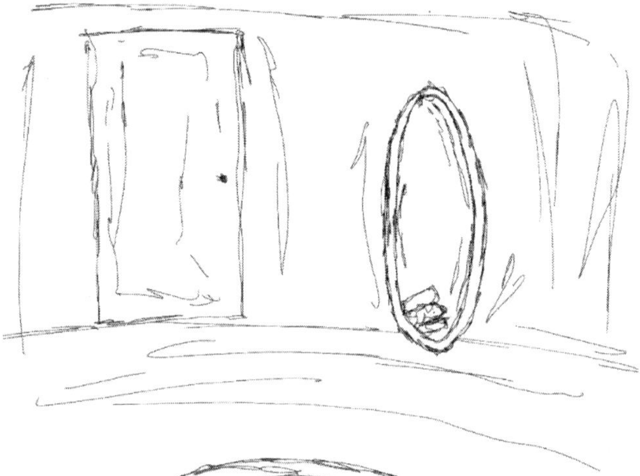

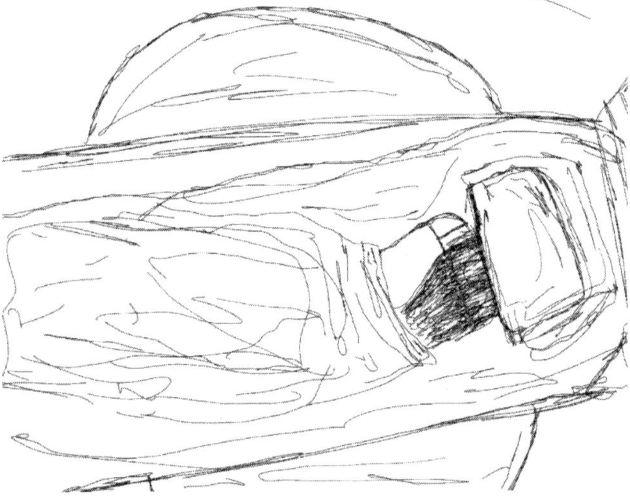

circling

I've always wondered what it would look like
Right before I fall
I've been doing well pondering life and its colors and
its skies
You dressed the room with baby blue and a hint of
lime
And I could be ashamed
Once dusk begins to decline
There are many moons at this hour
Or maybe it's just my eyes
The hands on the clock keep counting the time

I sip at my bottles; you count the stars that freckle the
sky
I've forgotten your name as the seconds or months or
years have gone by
Will it be erased come a rainy day,
Or will we take it to the grave?
Time knows no impatience, but I'll wait
The hands on the clock keep losing the time
But I'm going in circles

I've settled into my black,
Or my gray or my white
Whatever this is, it thickens every day
I'll be consumed the day before I die
And I wasn't afraid to make the change
I wasn't afraid to forget your name,
As those cruel hands keep counting the time
We're going in circles

I guess this is what it looks like
Right before I fall

spring cleaning

It's sunset time
The sun imprints on the wall
If I lived on good news, I wouldn't make it till the fall
I heard you made it out alive,
Or are you still walking that thread?
Every night I lay down on the couch
And try to forget

These days I'm never succeeding
Not with doing my best,
Not with handling my stress
And all I do is say sorry
But are the apologies real,
Or do I just say them in my head?

If I lived on good news, I wouldn't make it till the fall
I probably wouldn't even make it to my funeral
But when you get there, suit and tie,
Would you let me know if the sky's still blue?
I'm trying not to assume

And I used to be okay with staring

But then the ceiling got boring
And then I started yearning
For invisible things on the other side
When I make it there, too,
I'll let you know if the sky's still blue
I'll let you know that you're still my muse

And when I get comfortable, maybe I'll call
Open a cabinet or tilt the painting on the wall
Let you know I'm still listening
To your chest
When you think you stop breathing

It's sunset time
The sun imprints on the wall
Letting me know it's high tide tonight
And the ride might be bumpy after all

They say my soul is still lingering
I'll let you know when I find it

If I lived on good news, I wouldn't make it till the fall
But no worries; I'll be the wind in the trees
I'll watch the leaves change color,
And your voice doesn't sound the same
It was once summer rain and now it's thunder
I thought we weren't supposed to get these kinds of storms,
Be this kind of cold,

Until December

And these days I'm never succeeding
Not with doing my best,
Not with getting out of my head
But maybe I won't have to
If I get this place cleaned up by noon

And I used to be okay with staring
But then the ceiling got boring
And then I started yearning
For invisible things on the other side
But maybe if I did some spring cleaning
I'll let you know if the sky's still blue

SKINNY FAG ATTENTION-SEEKING
HORRIBLE SUPERFICIAL DRAMA QUEEN
VALUELESS   FAT
SLUT GOLD-DIGGING   BITCH   ORDINARY TERRIBLE
TRASHY PLASTIC WEAK LOUD REPLACEABLE STUPID
       WORTHLESS ARROGANT CHEAP WHORE
              UNNATURAL FEMINAZI   UGLY
                    EASY   INAPPROPRIATE
           BAD THOUGHTS

supernovas don't scare me anymore

Switches flip and things happen that you can't reverse
I just wish I would've told you all the things I never
said, but always meant, first
Truly, there's not a lot of them
There's not a lot I mean at all
Things are simple and ordered
And they're the things I hate the most
Coloring to me is bitter
I get points off for drawing outside the lines
Things that are simple and ordered
Are the things I most despise

Like lemonade in the summer
Or watching movies in the yard
Let's read a book on a rollercoaster
And try not to get paper cuts
Let's douse the living room in paint
And let the paint splatters be our furniture
I just wish I would've told you all the things I never
said, but always meant, first
Before there would be things that I'd wish to reverse

It's a short list,
The things I say versus the things I think
I haven't yet told my parents I'm not going to college
And I don't care if the tag says it's meant for men
I haven't yet figured out my identity
But I figure it's already been figured for me
I used to like sage and vanilla, but now I'm leaning towards auburn
Like a fiery sun
The sky is still blue, but supernovas don't scare me any more
And when the sky turns red, supernovas won't scare me any more

I have traveled at dusk through blackened streets
Looking for something good to eat
But the only offer was my own skin
So I shredded me apart
I had my doubts, but I tore me apart
And when the sun came and we all started over again,
I'd be the one in the alley
Feasting
On whatever I could reach
Whatever could reach me
It's only good manners
So I've been told

Our flesh and bone made to desire,
It's really no wonder why things get broke

We are made to destroy, aren't we?
Is that why supernovas don't scare me any more?
Is that why space doesn't scare me any more?
I'd never seen a sky so blue
Than the one I'd fallen from
But still as I was flying, I was homesick
But for nothing I can find
For nothing that can find me

You think you know all there is to know
But the truth is never subtle, never quiet
Always a drum in your ear, always loud
Everything is loud
And you were the loudest
But somehow I just
Didn't mind
I didn't mind at all
Are we bound for each other's destinations?
Have we already overlapped without our knowing?
Will I ever find you again?
The possibilities don't scare me any more
Supernovas don't scare me any more

For once I'll be true, my word
Or, rather, yours:
That was a goodbye kiss, wasn't it?
Maybe
But it's no bother to me

Now that I've said all I've never said, but always meant
That supernovas don't scare me any more
And when I was flying in the sky,
And never a sky so blue I'd seen,
Of all the loudness in the world,
The sky is much too quiet for me

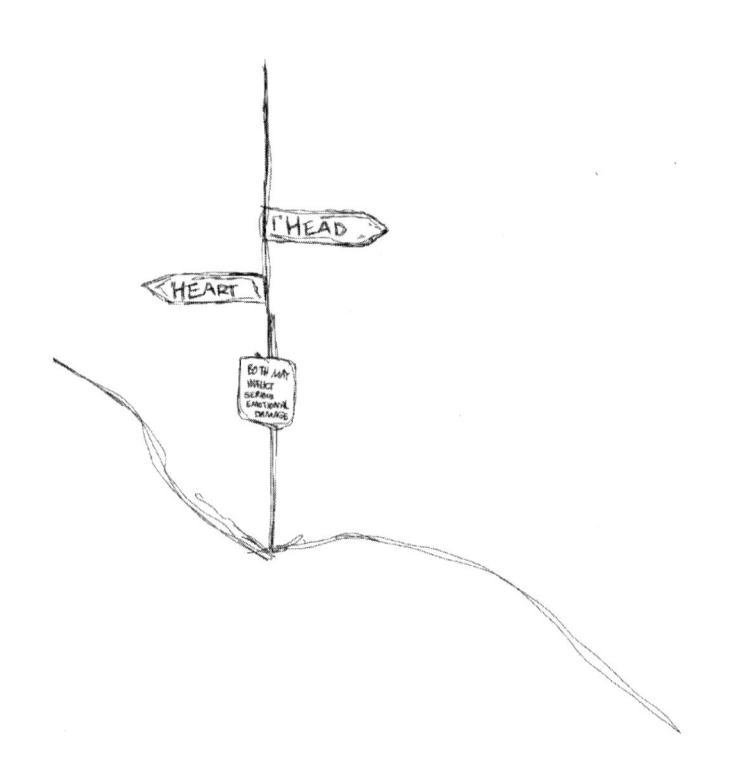

broken glass

My father taught me how to whistle,
But I've forgotten how
It was the same afternoon my mother left the clothes
on the line to dry
Your souls were glass; I crushed it
It's in the past, but I miss it
We so badly want the world in our hands
Until we have it
We long for its barren soil
Then neglect its flaws in total
And leave the symptoms in the sun to waste

You never know life till you're a minute from death
You never know yourself till you wrap the noose
around your neck
And perhaps it's better to be blissfully unaware
Dark and rapid and angry as you can be,
The sun is brighter in summer
But your smile is bigger in winter
And that's never something
I'll understand
Perhaps that's why when you longed for me,

I dropped your hand

Your souls were glass; I crushed it
It's in the past, but I miss it
We so badly want the world in our hands
Until we have it—
We long for July then are homesick for September
You long for one more day to remember
The very things you couldn't stand,
Like the whistles in the kitchen
It's in the past, but I miss it
You never know life till you're a minute from death

You tell me clip the clothes to the line,
But wring them out first—No, not like that
All the scolding, the yelling, the crying,
But in my head it's laughter
In my head, it's so much sweeter
In my head, all the things I remember
Are the things I wanted to forget

My father taught me how to whistle,
But I've forgotten how
And to put the kettle on the stove,
And to rinse the bowls,
And to hold my mother's hand
Dark and rapid and angry as you can be,
The sun is brighter in summer
But your smile is bigger in winter

And that's never something
I'll understand

We so badly want the world in our hands
Until we have it
We long for its barren soil
Then neglect its flaws in total
I miss it, but it's in the past
I wish there were no reflections in
Broken glass

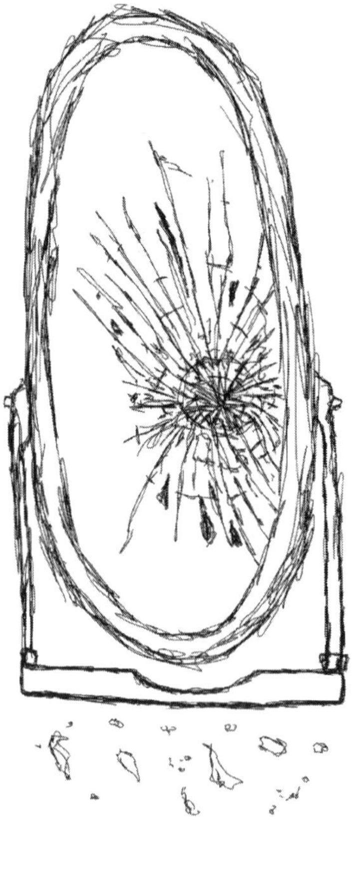

the ill-mannered gentleman

July nights are for fantasizing
About cutting my wrists
And not feeling empty
And not always running from something
I'm not sure exists

July afternoons are for planning my funeral
But funerals are for the living;
Just spread my ashes is all I ask
I wonder how it would feel to burn
Is it how I imagine it would be,
Still singing but just higher pitched,
So loud my eardrum splits?
In the summer heat I pour
The sweat and blood of my wrists

I long for the fantasy
To feel religion and empathy
Outside your bedroom walls
Your stripping me of my clothes
And my skin tender with bruises
Is how I feel respected,

Or did I just
Convince myself of it?

And I warned you, that I'm not good enough
That I've never been
And it was only a matter of time until it sunk beneath your skin
And it turns out
That waking up
To a dagger prodding at your throat
Is just as horrifying as you'd think it is

I betrayed this body
Letting you touch me
Letting you sink beneath my waves
And in the current, I betrayed my mind, too,
From all those nights I let you sleep in and stay
I betrayed my feelings, revealing them so deeply,
To someone who couldn't even buy
Even a false, surface respect
If it weren't for a needy, lonesome body,
You would've never met the right side of my bed

Most importantly, I betrayed myself,
My being so entirely,
Because I handed me over just like that
I betrayed myself more than anybody else had ever betrayed me

Now I don't have to wonder when you're coming back;
I don't deserve somebody to save me

I had to translate my soul to every other person I met,
But the ill-mannered gentleman is the one who speaks my language best
Most of our talking is against a wall, or hanging from the post of my bed,
But I'll still love the words that you said
As if you meant them

My fantasy is a broken dream, but so am I
Nothing has made me sadder than imagining myself never seeing you again;
And nothing has made me fall apart more than knowing you're perfectly fine with that

I would've gladly broken the clock to prove we were right on time
But you kept fixing the hands and taking all that was mine;
In fact, I never knew what was mine until you stole it
And I gave you my fingers, and I gave you my mouth,
But blood is the only aftertaste,
Now that I know what it's like
Spending a July night
Alone with a razor blade

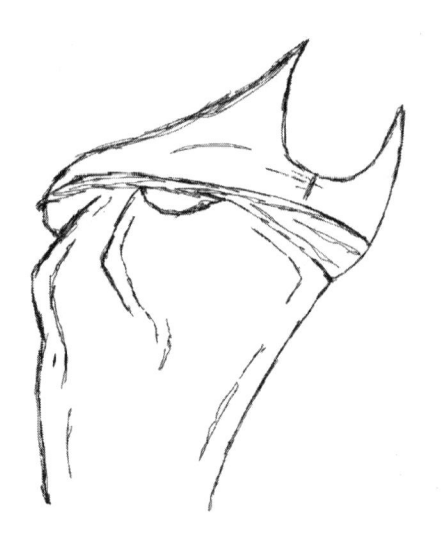

better

I hope I left more than the stain on your bedroom floor
Maybe a smudged fingerprint
From when I rummaged through your drawers
And the paint I picked off with my nails
And in your hairbrush, it's probably my hair

I think you might love me more now than you ever did then
You stole my pieces waiting for me to get spent
Now I have to rearrange with what I have left
Black is more comforting; in that we can agree
But I never thought you'd love the silhouette in the picture frames
More than me

It's a sickness I've never had,
One in which I'm not immune
We made each other bleed
And we tasted it
Just to know what we'd done
Like we couldn't live without it
And sometimes I smile thinking of the way

We both broke down that day
I guess that's why you don't fall in love with a masochist;
It's like going to church with two Catholics and an atheist
Don't give me the idea
To nail myself to a cross

You showed me the ropes and I strangled you here
And your voice in the morning is the bruises I bear
I guess that's why you don't fall in love with a masochist
I have too much fun making hell of it
Perhaps I'm the atheist

If you didn't love me then, I don't think you'll ever love me again
Because I'm getting better
I'm trying to get better
I'm washing the stains and I'm cleaning my blood
But I'm not cured yet
There's still some of you left
And sometimes when I run the shower
I think of every hour
I wasted on you
And sometimes when I think I'm not growing
I think back to the moments
The bruises in the morning,

The way you taste,
Like drying leaves and dying seeds,
It made me sicker
And maybe I'll come running back when my skin's thicker
But something tells me
That's just not how you get better
I'll find a new address to send my love letters

I think you might love me now more than you ever did then
You stole my pieces waiting for me to get spent
Now I have to rearrange with what I have left
Black is more comforting; in that we can agree
But I never thought you'd love the silhouette in the picture frames
More than me

I guess that's why you don't fall in love
With a masochist

THE HOLY BIBLE (OR WHATEVER)

patience

I still watch you moving for miles
As if you're the ripples in the sea
Like you're the circling of a tide
At the bottom of a swimming pool
And you breathe your words of anger,
So luscious and obscure,
Like the talons of an eagle
Like a living soul to be mourned

Fire
You're lost in a fire with liberty
Moving like iron swept in the sea
You're sitting at the bottom, stubborn and idle
And I'll be waiting patiently
For your return
For your return

Maybe when the trees grow thinner limbs
And the leaves change colors again
You'll emerge
Patience
Patience is a virtue, you see,

That's what you would say
With all your fearless audacity

Fire
You're lost in a fire with liberty
You're sinking so effortlessly
Moving like iron, growing in fire
Like surface tension
The ripples at the top are steep
And unrelenting,
Just like you
At the bottom

I
I see a soul so flickering
Like the swaying of a willow tree
The measure of movement so randomly
And I
I want to know what's underneath
The water was clear but now it's sickly green
I wonder if I know
Of your savior

Fire
You're lost in a fire of scrutiny
All the dirty eyes watching
Burying their sins in their trench coats
They've brought a camera and prepare a rose
For when the traffic in your lungs collapse

And puddles
Are mere decoration
Like a flickering chandelier in an abandoned dungeon
Adding insult to injury
You've traveled so far from where you sleep

Fire
You're lost in a fire with liberty
Moving like iron swept in the sea
You're sitting at the bottom, stubborn and idle
And I'll be waiting patiently
For your return
For your return

the chain

There are some things that are easier to experience
Than to admit
Like when your doctor is staring at you
And praying you didn't do it
But you tried
Didn't get that far though
My brother was in the shower
So I couldn't get inside
But I wanted to
I just wanted to see what it felt like
Or at least that's what I tell myself
But I know
I wanted more than the feeling
I wanted to finally feel nothing at all

And I think for the rest of my life
I'm gonna be chained to you
I'm never gonna look at shaving razors the same way
And every time I step into a bathroom,
I'll taunt myself
And I'm scared
That one day I'll finally fall through

That one day I'll break the chain
And do what you want me to

And I'm sorry
I know you depend on my openness
But things were much easier to admit
Back then
And I'm struggling
With saying the words
With feeling the hurt
All over again
I thought I was done with my dark times
So why does this feel like the darkest I've ever known?
I thought I had broken the chain a long time ago
But know you're back
When it's convenient for you

And I'm sorry
I'm doing it all over again
But this time my anxiety
Just isn't stopping me
And that's what scares me
Take my scissors and my razors
Don't let me out the front door
Ever again
Because I'm tainted
And the world is already so contaminated
It doesn't need me to add to the flavorless anticipation
That one day I'll finally break the chain

And do what you want me to

It's been six years and hundreds of tears
And thousands of hours lying in bed
And millions of words I've written to try to get over it
But it just keeps crawling back and it knows me more each time
And I'm terrified

I don't know where I'm going,
Nor do I know where I belong
So the streets I'm turning down,
Are they leading me to succumb,
Or am I finally
Stepping outside the realm
Where I can feel like myself,
Whatever I am any more?

There are things that are easier to experience
Than to admit
Like when your doctor is staring at you
And praying you didn't do it
But you tried
Didn't get that far though
My brother was in the shower
So I couldn't get inside
But I wanted to
I just wanted to see what it felt like
Or at least that's what I tell myself

But I know
I wanted more than the feeling
I want to finally feel nothing at all

And I think for the rest of my life
I'm gonna be chained to you
I'm never gonna look at shaving razors the same way
And every time I step into a bathroom,
I'll taunt myself
And I'm scared
That one day I'll finally fall through
That one day I'll break the chain
And do what you want me to

IT'S
HIS
FAULT

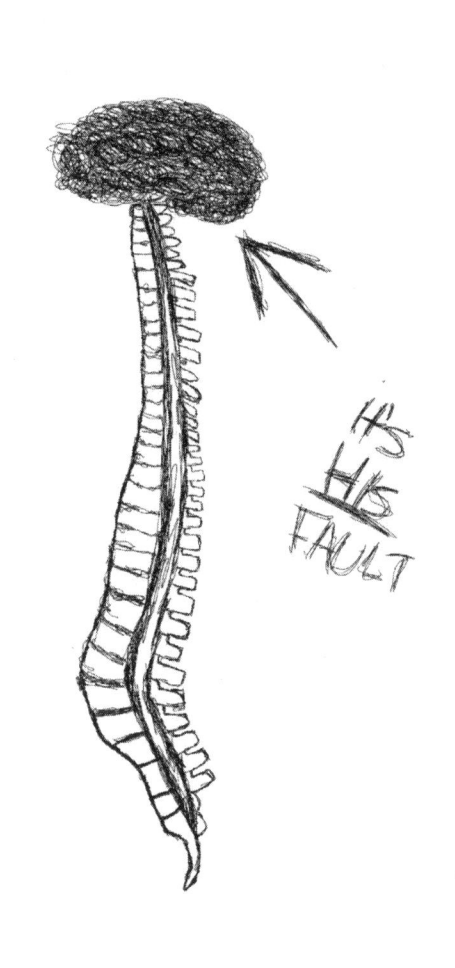

yellow

Please,
don't find in a second
what I have spent my entire life looking for.
Please,
struggle as I did.
I need to validate myself after
all this time of meeting a peace
that wanders every time I come near,
and surviving a life in the broom closet of a kingdom,
washing myself clean with an empty soap bottle,
in a clogged sink,
and treading the excess waters in fresh socks.

Please,
don't find in a second
what I have spent my entire life looking for.
Please,
struggle as I did.
You left your camera in my car
and now all the pictures are of you.
They say you just know it when you know it,
when your heart is beating slow;

you just know it when you know it,
when they're walking down your road;
you just know it when you know it,
when you feel them getting close
to home.

But please,
don't find in a second
what I have spent my entire life looking for.
Please,
struggle as I did.
And just know when you open up my door,
you're the worn-out recording of my favorite song—
you never stop playing, because you never leave my
head.
And just know when you open up my door,
I'm not ready to be left.

Please,
don't find in a second
what I have spent my entire life looking for.
Please,
struggle as I did.
I need to validate myself after
all this time of meeting a peace
that wanders every time I come near,
and surviving a life in the broom closet of a kingdom,
washing myself clean with an empty soap bottle,
in a clogged sink,

and treading the excess waters in fresh socks.

In the battle, we're both opposite colors of the flames.
No, I am not the maid; unfortunately, I am the queen,
with a heart of red,
a love gone yellow,
and orange for a home.

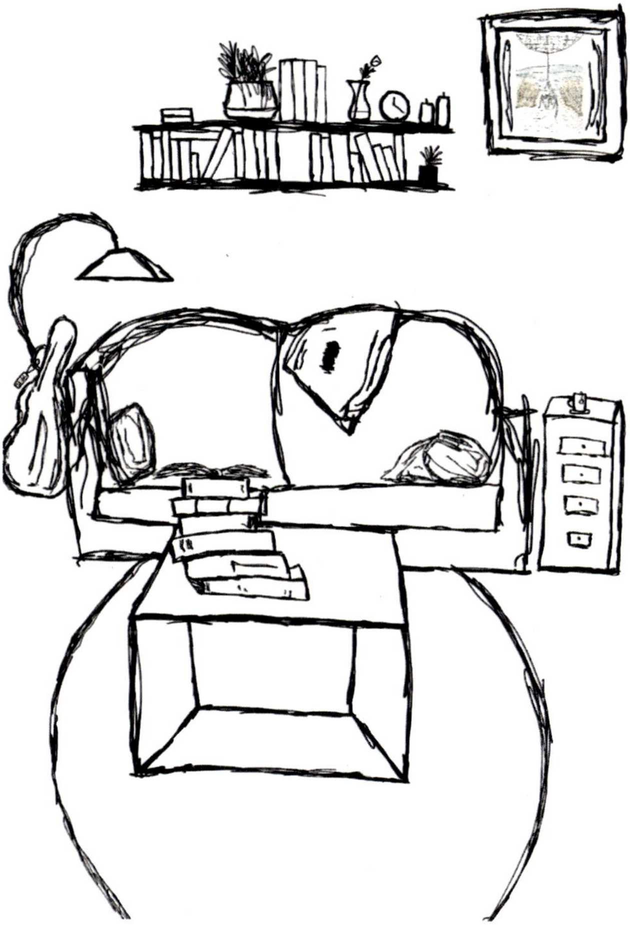

an inch of religion

you never know yourself until part of you dies
and the rest just rots away
like how everything was fascinating,
especially how i can lose my patience like a spider on the wall
or a cat's whisker that nips at my cheek
it gnaws at me constantly
i wonder where my patience went

when everything was fascinating
when i had the focus to sit and learn and write
i know i'm better off without it
but all i do is write about it,
every bad habit i ever had
to own the fact
that nothing's fascinating any more
or maybe it is but my eyes are still glued shut
and i can't relinquish fear without kicking up dust
and i'll never ever be patient again

when everything was fascinating
and every person was worth the waiting

and i could sleep a full night without waking
and not be dreaming conversations
that make my reality so full of hatred
maybe everything's fascinating but i can't see it yet
maybe i'm old sand that hasn't yet met the sun
and maybe i'm prettier in the mirror than in my head
or maybe i'll wake up without wondering if i'll ever do it again
the scribblings on the backdrop—
it's all white, it's all clean, everything is fascinating
but then my ink, it all pours out
i take my calloused hands and i spread it around
it stains, it bruises, it scars, but it'll never fade
it'll only worsen with time like how i've worsened with age

and like the bottles underneath the seat,
the socks in the dryer,
every little thing i've ever had—
it all leaves wistfully
and my touch is vermilion scars underneath
the sun does burn but so does black
a hand is pulling me to open my eyes
i just hope it's worth the six years of my time,
like driving the miles to come home
and the books are gone from the shelves—
you knew what i believed in,
you knew it's what i needed,
and so you packed them all in boxes and away

like a fair rhythm void of rhyme,
you embrace both the wound and the remedy
the nights, the mornings, the long afternoons
could have all been voided
had i not been yearning for a book gone from my shelf

i wish i could record my dreams and rewatch them
to prove all my fantasies are never mine alone
and i know i'm better off without it
but all i do is write about it
i'm remorseful to a god
i don't believe in

the ink is smudging on my clothes
and a hand is pulling me to open my eyes

hiding places

I know this road
And I remember exactly why
I know those books on the shelf;
They never looked so white
They were smudged with prints
And tearing tape
From all the kids
Trying to find their way
From all the kids who sat in the back,
Plotting their escape
You can find them where the light is,
Drawing pictures and stealing stars with their moon-catching nets
You can find them where the light is,
Singing songs to themselves all out of pitch

The dogs know their routines
They come to my room to flee
How sad is it
That we are kids
With hiding places?

I miss sitting alone in the back of the library,
Reading Shel Silverstein, thinking pretty
I know these books were on the shelf;
They never looked so white
I bought you brand new copies
With these books, you'll see the light
Be sad, be happy, take the pancake from the middle of the stack
Be bad, be tacky, be everyone you ever wanted to have back

I read Shel Silverstein
Because the dogs know their routines
They come to my room to flee
How sad is it
That we are kids
With hiding places?

How sad is it
That we are kids
With bruised souls
Yet happy faces?

Play tug o' war and hug o' war
Put something good in the world
That wasn't there before
And colors
Black and red and blue
Apple green and aquamarine

And nothing before you've ever seen

You look worse in the light
But don't we all
Do it away with the creams and supplements and pills
And nothing you ever asked for
To sit under the bed
And wait in the closet
For apple green and aquamarine
To visit you in happy dreams

You'll find me where the light is,
Drawing pictures and stealing stars with my moon-catching net
You'll find me where the light is,
Singing songs to myself all out of pitch
And nothing I ever wanted
Was everything I needed—
Apple green and aquamarine—
To put something in the world
It's never seen

Oh, how sad is it
That we are kids
With hiding places?

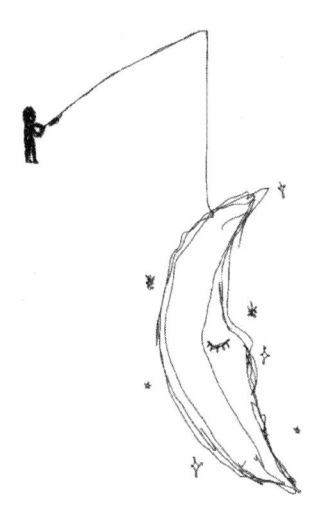

seasons

Keep a little fire burning
It gets cold here without you
I can't walk through a wood
Not illuminated by dawn
And I will walk with you for as long as you will let me
I will run to you, for as long as time will let me

You say,
Dawn will come
And I will greet it when it does
But where will you be?
Please don't
Get swept up by the sea;
I know how easily it can happen
When we were eighteen, and we were free,
Would you still have let it happen?

I say,
I will be the dawn overlooking your tide
If you wash away,
I'll be the morning sky
I can't

Walk through a wood
Not illuminated by dawn
I'll walk with you until the dawn has come
And I will walk with you long after

They say,
If a man writes you a few poems,
He loves you
But if he writes you a few hundred poems, he loves
Writing poems
Well, I love you with every ripple in the sea
But if less means more,
Then I'll write a few poems less than the waves
That bring you to me

You say,
Do fret none when the sun hasn't come;
We are just as well in the rain
But I can't
Walk through a wood
Not illuminated by dawn
Will it be your hand or a fire that guides me?
It'll be your hand and its fire that guides me

Dawn will come
And I will greet it when it does
I'll walk with you until the dawn has come
And I'll walk with you long after
No need

For flames upon this beach
So long as we have each other

Flower-strewn and sandy feet,
We were eighteen and free
And I will still run to you for as long as time will let me

There is no greater crime I will ever commit with you
Than this treason
This is the end of a love, my dear,
Or the change of a season

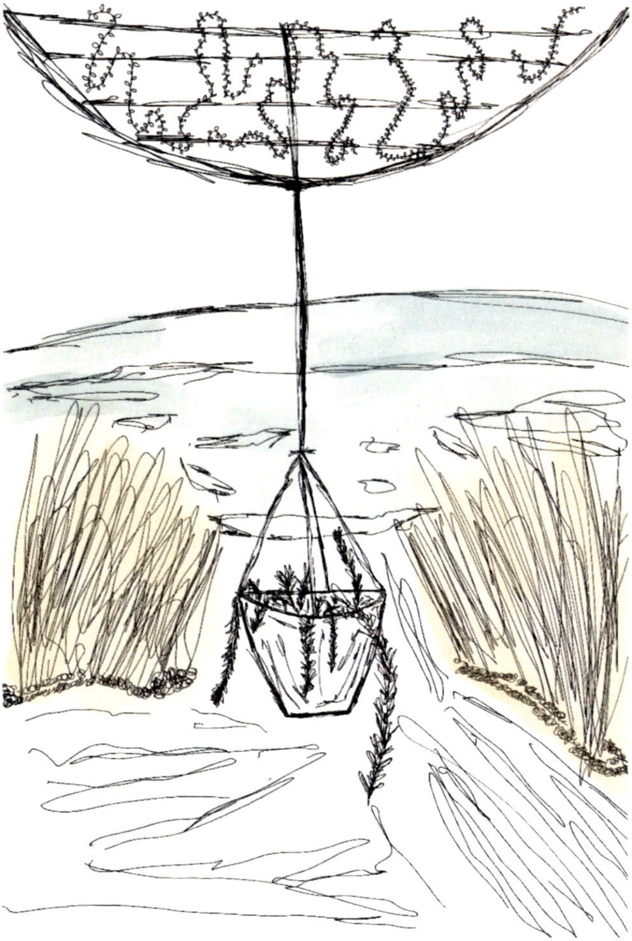

papa's poem (bonus)

You'll find me at the end of the rainbow
I won't be the pot of gold; I'll be the land
That brought you there, only to disappoint

I'll be the flowers in the grass you don't see,
But other people say they're there
Other people say I'm there

I'll be the hands that held me and the hands that destroyed me

I'll be the man who never sang a song into his lover's mouth,
Who only ever learned to say what they say,
But never what they mean

If it rains and I drown, and I leave the people I love,
I at least didn't know the true depths of myself until I loved them with all I am

I ask my sunshine boy to tell me I'm here, tell me I'm alive

He doesn't know what it means
He'll know when I'm the tide washing him inshore,
To lose every battle he's ever fought
He'll know when I'm the sickness to drive him to hell

You'll be my dictionary and I'll be the one word in the
billions you just don't like

'Tis morning now;
'Tis time I be a tide

'Tis morning now, sunshine boy;
I'll be the morning tide

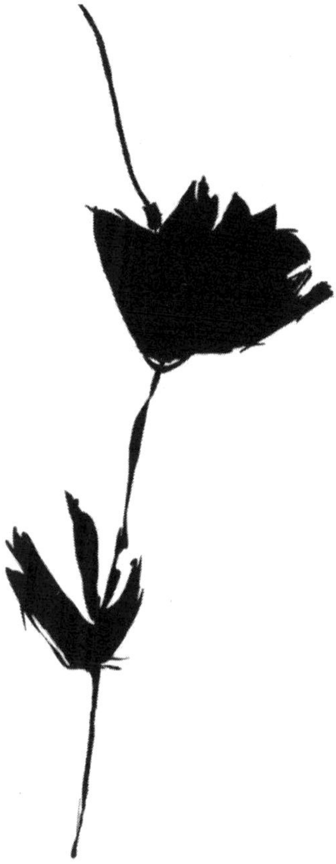

FEELING SUICIDAL?

National Suicide Prevention Hotline: 1-800-273-8255 / 988
National Mental Illness Hotline: 1-800-950-6264
Dating Abuse and Domestic Violence Hotline: 1-866-331-9474
Sexual Assault Hotline: 1-800-656-4673
National Eating Disorder Hotline: 1-800-931-2237
Bullying Hotline: 1-800-420-1479
Transgender Suicide Hotline: 877-565-8860
The Trevor Project (suicide hotline for LGBTQIA+ youths): 866-488-7386
Self-Harm Hotline: 1-800-DONT-CUT / 1-800-344-HELP
Runaway Hotline: 1-800-843-5200 / 1-800-843-5678
Depression Hotline: 1-630-482-9696
General Crisis Text Line: Text SUPPORT to 741-741
Abuse Hotline: 1-800-799-7233 / 1-800-787-3224
Addiction Hotline: 800-910-3734
Exhale (post-abortion hotline/pro-voice): 1-866-439-4235
Poison Control: 1-800-222-1222

Giving to other people helps me feel better. If you would like to:

Text ENOUGH / FLOYD to 55156 to sign a Color of Change petition
Text JUSTICE to 668366 to sign a MoveOn petition
Sign a petition at JusticeForBigFloyd
Donate to the Black Lives Matter Movement
Volunteer or apply for an internship with the National Alliance on Mental Illness (NAMI)
Volunteer and donate to the Trevor Project
Donate to the Human Rights Campaign
Donate to UNICEF
Donate to the ASPCA
Donate to support Ukraine humanitarian aid
Donate to support Israel/Palestine humanitarian aid
Donate to support Lebanon's aid
Support Nigeria and *End SARS*, a movement against police brutality in Nigeria